G000134869

PLEASE OBSERVE T[

If no pavement on highway
Walk on the RIGHT HAND SIDE of the road
FACING the oncoming traffic
Guard against all risk of fire
Fasten ALL GATES
Keep dogs under control
Avoid damaging fences, hedges & walls
Leave no LITTER
Safe guard water supplies
Protect wildlife, plants & trees

take nothing but photographs
leave nothing but footpaths
kill nothing but time

The walks in this book have been researched and walked by Joy & Charles Boldero. Wherever possible they are being continually updated.

All the walks are over public footpaths, bridleways, tracks & country lanes with a good hostelry (Pub or Inn) recommended for a welcome pint of real ale and good food. The book also includes details of the old uses of some of the wild flowers found on route and names of the birds such as avocets & marsh harriers that can be spotted on the marshes & creeks; and it gives historic information regarding the places visited on the walks.

BOOKS PUBLISHED BY JOY & CHARLES BOLDERO

CHRONICLE OF A NORFOLK VILLAGE - THURNING

CIRCULAR WALKS IN NORFOLK

MORE CIRCULAR WALKS IN NORFOLK

COASTAL CIRCULAR WALKS IN NORFOLK

WEAVERS WAY CIRCULAR WALKS

LONG WALKS IN NORFOLK WITH JOY & CHARLES BOLDERO'S FAVOURITE PUBS

CYCLE RIDES IN NORFOLK

DISCOVER NORFOLK WITH OUR CIRCULAR DRIVES

JOY BOLDERO 'TALKS' ABOUT WALKING & THE COUNTRYSIDE

WEAVERS WAY
CIRCULAR WALKS

Published & Distributed by Joy & Charles
Boldero, Thurning, Norfolk, February 1990.
Front Cover by Mike Bignold, Thurning.
Photographs by Charles Boldero

British Library Cataloguing in Publication Data.
Boldero Joy 1938 -
Circular Walks in Norfolk
Vol 1
1. Norfolk. Visitors' guides
1 Title 11, Boldero, Charles 1924 -
ISBN 0 9515478 4 4

Weavers Way is one of the four long distance paths in Norfolk, its whole length is 56 miles long. This book contains 12 circular walks around Weavers Way. The other long distance paths are Peddars Way which starts at Thetford and takes you to the coast at Holme-next-the-Sea, then the coastal path travels on to Cromer, where Weavers Way starts and from Great Yarmouth, Angles Way takes you back to Thetford, about a total of 220 miles.

This book describes circular walks around Weavers Way starting at the attractive seaside town of Cromer on the north Norfolk coast.
The walks takes you through two stately homes owned by the National Trust, also through pretty villages, along tracks, country lanes and footpaths ending at Great Yarmouth on the east Norfolk coast.

It goes along the old Muddle and Go Nowhere railway line This is the name the locals fondly gave to the M.& G.N. lines that linked most of Norfolk to-gether giving the county an excellent public transport system. It also connected up with lines going to the north of England and London. However the wisdom of Beeching destroyed all that in the 1950's and left Norfolk bereft of a public transport system and the car or horse are the only means of transport for the majority of those who live in the rural countryside of Norfolk!

INDEX

INDEX

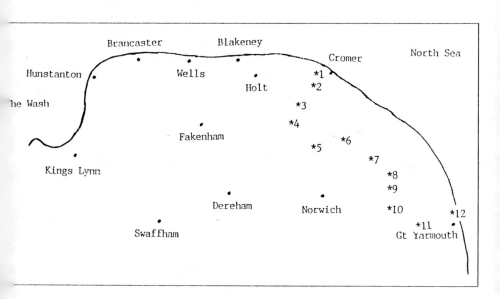

THE MAPS IN THIS BOOK ARE DIAGRAMMATIC AND NOT STRICTLY TO SCALE

------- PATH   _ _ _ TRACK   _____ ROAD

7 MILES

This is a lovely walk with very little road walking. The only pub close to the route is the White Horse Inn in West Street, Cromer near the car park, but there are numerous places in the town that serve food.

START WALK The walk starts from the Meadow Road car park in Cromer. From the car park turn left then bear left at the road junction. Continue along this road with Cromer Hall on right.

This Gothic knapped flint house was built for George Thomas Windham in 1827. It was used for the I.T.V. serial the 'Black Tower' starring Roy Marsden.

Just after lodge & red tiled house turn right at footpath sign continuing along Weavers Way. We suggest you use the left hand path at edge of field, then half way up by two trees turn right, then at footpath sign turn left to top of wood.

Go diagonally across field to railway bridge. Cross bridge then keep straight ahead at edge of field ignoring the track rightish and follow this path around the woodland to road. Turn right along road.

The woodland that lies both sides of the road is cared for by the Woodland Trust and members of the public are welcome to walk round the woodland paths.

Turn left at Weavers Way sign along a narrow path. The path widens then becomes a rough track. At the road turn right then go down track keeping war memorial and green on your right. Continue along the track until you reach the small gate into field.

1

Leave Weavers Way (which goes off left) and go across large meadow to gate. Go through small gate & turn left up tarmac drive ignoring all turns to left & right. Pass Felbrigg Hall on right.

This 17th century house was built for Thomas Windham. It is now owned by the National Trust and open to the public from about Easter time to October, except Tuesdays & Fridays. The house & gardens are well worth a visit. There is also a cafe here for refreshments but please check leaflets regarding time of openings.

Go through gate and keep along driveway and entrance gate. Turn left along country lane.Turn right at the road junction walking into Aylmerton..

Turn right at junction. There are fifty species of wild flowers growing in the churchyard. The Saxon church itself is worth visiting. The rood screen dates from 1445 when John Baker left 10s (50p) to the church fabric.

The screen at one time had a loft. The church also has a fine altar amongst its many gems.

Just after the church turn left (yellow marker on Electric pole & gate post) Go through white gate and into field. Follow the line of the footpath sign (on inside of tree hedge) across the field. At second field turn left & walk right around the pig field to white post in hedge gap. At the third field walk diagonally across the field aiming for a single white post in hedge line midway between two electric poles. Go diagonally over fourth field again aiming for white posts in hedge line. Continue straight across fifth field to stile which is to the left-hand side of the field. Climb stile and cross meadow (The cows with their curious nature are friendly !).

Climb stile. Turn right along main road. Turn left at footpath sign just after "Woodlands" along edge of field At the end of tree/hedge line continue straight across field to wood.

Go through wood, ignore paths to left and right Go around barrier and straight across cross tracks keeping the National Trust stone collecting box on left. This area is covered with heather and gorse. Keep along main path as it descends then rises then descends again. Continue along this path through the natural woodland, ignore paths to right and left.

Continue down along narrow path beside houses with field on left. At the rough track keep right. At the end of Calves Well Lane cross road and go along track opposite with commemorate seat dedicated to James Sainty who did so much in his lifetime for the villages of East & West Runton.

When the path becomes a tarmac one turn left then immediately right uphill with fingerpost with 'no horse' sign on it. Keep along the edge of fence line. Gorse and broom with their bright yellow flowers grow in abundance here as does honeysuckle

There are fine views of the coastline over the golf course. The path descends. At hard path turn left then immediately take narrow path on right by white footpath sign.

Continue along this tree lined path to T junction then turn left uphill across common. At the top of the hill there are fine views of Cromer and the coast.

Go down steps then across field on well defined path. Ignore path to right and at junction of tracks turn right going downhill under a canopy of trees. Cross road keeping the Green on left.

Keep straight ahead along road then just before the 30 mile an hour signs turn left up signed track/driveway. Keep towards bungalow and go along very narrow footpath leftish between fences.

Go through gate and cross railway line with care, **STOP - LOOK -LISTEN**. Go through gate and turn left along the field edge. Keep on this footpath to wood then field edge. Cross tarmac track, take signed narrow path between trees. Keep straight along edge of field then take the left-hand edge of field with wall on left. At the track turn left. Cross road and continue along track, turn right passing the mushroom farm on right.

At the end of Sandy Lane turn left and continue along the pavement turning right then left back to the car park and start of walk.

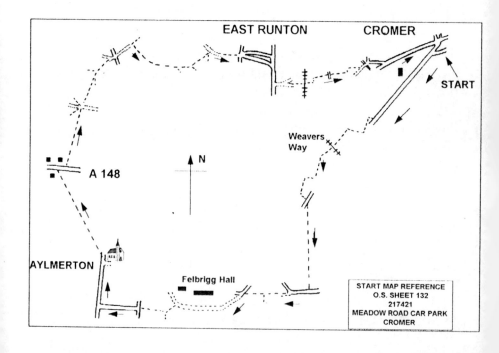

EAST RUNTON

CROMER

START

Weavers Way

N

A 148

AYLMERTON

Felbrigg Hall

START MAP REFERENCE
O.S. SHEET 132
217421
MEADOW ROAD CAR PARK
CROMER

METTON

3 1/2 MILES

This is a lovely rural walk and it starts at the church at Metton where there is limited parking. Metton is situated 1 mile west of the A140 at Roughton which is 3 miles south of Cromer.

There are many birds and wild flowers to be seen on this walk. The only place for refreshments is Felbrigg Hall. On the lake in the Hall grounds water fowl, including Egyptian geese which have a distinguishing eye marking can be seen. Pheasants, especially the cock birds with their splendid colourful plumage, wander in and out of the woods.

The 14th century flint church at Metton which has stone quoins and dressings is well worth visiting. It has in its east window 16th century Flemish glass and just inside the door hangs a painted Parish Constable staff made in the time of William IV.

START WALK With the church and war memorial behind you walk westwards along the tree lined country lane, crossing a stream.

Turn left along the Sustead road. At footpath sign turn right over plank bridge and follow path with yellow marker signs around the edges of the fields to road.

At the country lane turn right. In October and November the trees are beautiful with their autumn colourings. The old board school on left built in 1875 has been well restored and is now a Field Study Centre.

Cross road and go through small gate with the lodge house on left. Continue along track and after about 150 yards turn right to wooden fence and stile, climb stile.

Walk across the large meadow aiming for the church. Among these meadows there are fine views of Felbrigg Hall and the lake, which was given to the National Trust by the distinguished author R.W. Ketton-Cremer.

Go over stream and continue uphill over the meadow to stile. Climb stile and go along well defined path around the field.

Climb stile and go into churchyard. Follow the path around the east end of the church.

The 13th century church has some excellent brasses on its floor. It has a fine roof and boxed pews and is stepped in history.

Go through gate, turn right and walk along the path at edge of field.

At the track turn right along Weavers Way.

Go through gate which has Weavers Way signs and over the path across the field. Climb stile and continue along path at edge of woodland. The path then goes along the edge of a field and further along over the middle of it.

Climb stile then go diagonally left over the field following the Weavers Way signs. Go over the bridge and stile and continue along path over meadow.

Climb several stiles (at end of each field) and finally go through the churchyard. Climb stile and cross the road to start of walk.

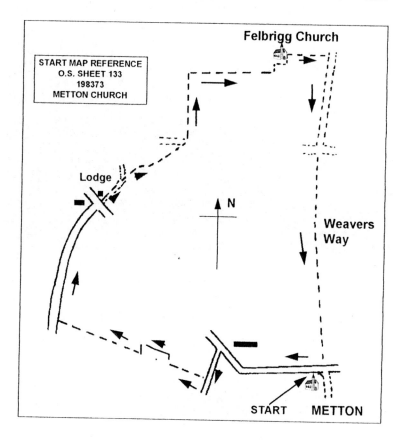

START MAP REFERENCE
O.S. SHEET 133
198373
METTON CHURCH

Felbrigg Church

Lodge

N

Weavers
Way

START   METTON

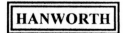

HANWORTH

4 MILES

There is free parking on the large common in the very attractive village of Hanworth. Hanworth is situated about 4 miles south of Cromer and 1 mile west of the A140 Cromer to Norwich road.

START WALK With the common on left and the wood on the right walk towards the white gate. Go over cattle grid and continue along the country lane.

To the right Hanworth Hall comes into view. This lovely 18th century house was built by Robert Doughty. In 1884 it was sold to the Windham family who owned Felbrigg Hall. It is said that there is a chestnut tree in the grounds with a girth of 29 feet 7 inches!

Turn right at the church along a wide rough track with Weavers Way sign. The footpath curves left between woodland.

Continue along track past the buildings of Manor Farm. Turn right along wide grass track opposite the white Alby Farm notice. When the track ends go slightly left across the field to a tree lined grassy lane.

At the end of the lane turn right into a tarmac lane. Turn left into another country lane and at the road turn right. Turn left into another country lane with letter box on right.

Continue along this tree lined country lane. There are fine views of the countryside along here and in the banks the tall pink flowered campion is found. Both the white and pink campion are scentless. In the hedges the dog rose grows. It is so named because the ancient Greeks thought the roots would cure a bite from a mad dog. In the past children drank a syrup made from the rose hips because it was rich in vitamin C.

Turn right immediately after the cottage by a wire fence line along a defined path at edge of field. Cross the stream by the wooden bridge with the old Mill house on left. At the lane turn right.

At the T junction turn right. This leads to the attractive village of Aldborough. On the green cricket is still played in the summer months. The village sign depicts on one side of it the tanning industry that once thrived here, and in 1845 it is recorded that there was a tanner, currier, saddler and fellmonger business in the village. A fellmonger dealt in sheepskins.

The other side of the sign shows the famous stock fairs that have been held on the green in midsummer for over 700 years.
The friendly BLACK BOYS Inn serves excellent meals at lunch time and in the evening.

Opposite the Inn turn right along the Hanworth road. At the
footpath sign immediately before the Post Office shop turn left.
The path narrows between trees. Cross stream by the bridge then
go along the edge of the field.

Climb stile and cross the meadow to second stile. Turn right at the
country lane, then left at the bridleway sign by Thurgarton Lodge.
Go along the tree lined track.

Many wild flowers grow along here and that in turn attracts the
brown and wall butterflies. Flowers such as scabious with its lilac
blue flowers, harebells with their dainty blue flowers and
hardheads that have knob like pinky flowers can be seen.

At the country lane turn right and continue along the road until
you reach the common at Hanworth and the start of the walk.

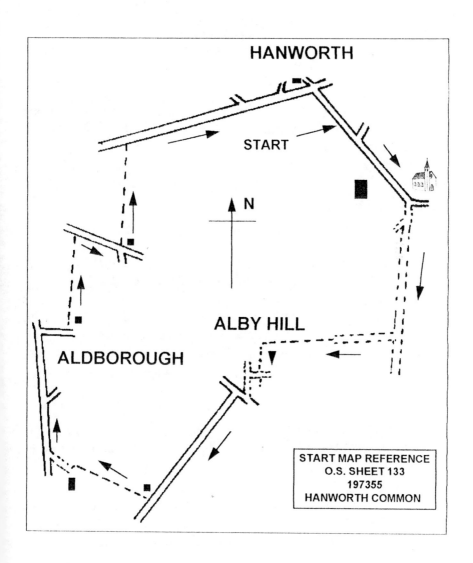

HANWORTH

START

↑ N

ALBY HILL

ALDBOROUGH

START MAP REFERENCE
O.S. SHEET 133
197355
HANWORTH COMMON

4 MILES

This walk starts at Thwaite Common which is situated near Erpingham, 6 miles south of Cromer, Just off the A140. There is limited free parking on and near the common.
This is a pleasant walk where many wild flowers are found and the Spread Eagle Arms is well known for its variety of real ales and good food.

START WALK Keeping the common and pond on right go up the country lane past pretty flint cottages. Turn left at Weavers Way sign up going up the track between house and barns.

Along this winding path there are fine views of the countryside. Wild tansy with its bright yellow flower can be found along here. At one time cooks used tansy and at Easter tansy cake was a favourite. It was said that its strong taste kept the mice away from the corn and flies away from the meat.

At the end of the track turn left then left again at the road. Turn right at Weavers Way sign going down the lane and after walking about 200 yards turn left down tree lined Pack Lane.

Campion grows in profusion along here and cow parsley which has a distinctive odour and whose frothy lace like flowers gave it the name of 'Queen's Anne's lace'. Country children at one time made pea-shooters out of the hollow stems. There are several crab apple trees along here. Birds love the fruit of these trees; in days gone by the fermented juice was used for scalds and sprains.

Turn left into a track and left again at the T junction. Turn right at the country road then left with post box on right.

At the end of this country lane cross the road and go over bank and field opposite. Climb bank at yellow marker and cross second field aiming to the left of the house amongst the trees. Climb stile and walk along the driveway. Reaching the country lane turn right.

Continue along this road to Erpingham. At T junction turn left. About 150 yards to the right is the 16th century Spread Eagle Arms where tasty meals can be obtained as well as a variety of real ales to choose from.

Erpingham is named after Sir Thomas Erpingham whose family were landowners as far back as the 14th century. In 1665 there was a terrible thunderstorm and a fireball killed a man in the village.
Just after the Ark Restaurant turn left down a narrow path with Weavers Way sign. Climb stiles and a plank bridge. Go over the common aiming diagonally for the fence line on right. Keeping the fence line on right continue along the path. climb stile and aim for second stile. Continue along the country road back to start of walk.

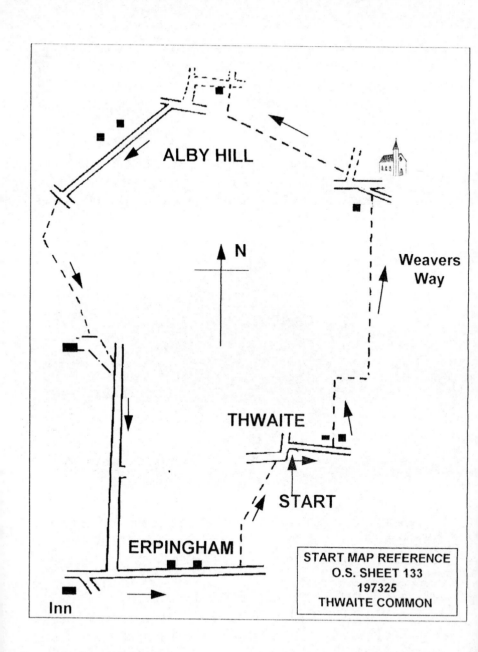

ALBY HILL

N

Weavers
Way

THWAITE

START

ERPINGHAM

Inn

START MAP REFERENCE
O.S. SHEET 133
197325
THWAITE COMMON

FELMINGHAM

5 MILES

There is a free car park at the old station in Felmingham. The village is situated on the B1145 2 miles west of North Walsham. Take the Skeyton turning from the B1145 in the village and follow the road around until you see the Weavers Way car park sign. There is no pub in Felmingham but several places in North Walsham where good food is served.

START WALK From the car park walk towards the old railway line and turn right. This area has been designated a special reserve for butterflies.

Gate keeper, meadow brown, small skipper and ringlet are just a few of the variety of butterflies that can be seen here. Flowers such as heathers, hardheads, tree lupin and rosebay willowherb grow in profusion along the track as well as many species of trees.

Keep along Weavers Way. Go through gate, cross the road and continue along the footpath opposite. The path crosses a river and immediately after going under a road bridge turn left up a steep bank to the road.

Turn left along this country lane, then right along a rough track between fields. Turn sharp left with barn ahead passing between a house on left and barns on right. Follow the main track as it bears right up to Mill Road.

Turn left along the road then right at footpath sign. turn right at main road.

Further along take the Suffield road to the left. At T junction turn right. Just after Oak Farm Cottage turn left keeping hedge on left.

Continue straight across the field on the wide path, keeping the bank on left. At the end of the boundary go over the bank and continue along the field edge in second field with hedge on left.
At end go over the bank and turn right along a short track and at the road turn left. Walk through Felmingham village with its attractive village sign on the green.

Where the road bends sharply left turn right along the Skeyton road.

The church, which always flies the English flag from its tower, is worth visiting. Around the south door are six stone carved faces. The church has a fine roof and the font is 13th century. In 1742 the building was burnt down except for the tower. It was rebuilt and re-opened in 1754.

Turn right into Elaine Road, then left into Sharon Close, then almost immediately right into a narrow footpath between fence and trees.

Cross field and at the hedge turn left keeping the hedge on right. At the end of the hedge keep straight across the field. At the country lane turn right and walk about 100 yards then turn left where the bank ends and where there is a division of crops. There are fine views of the countryside along here.

Go across the field. Go down steep bank onto Weavers Way and turn left. Turn left again into the car park and start of walk.

The name Felmingham is said to have derived from Feolma's people - the 'ham' means a homestead of Feolma's people. In 1381 there was a peasants revolt. The leader, John Litester, a dyer, had a house in Felmingham. He led 50,000 labourers, the reason for the revolt was increase in taxes from 4d to 1 shilling (5P) a 300% rise. They fled for sanctuary in the parish church. However the warlike Bishop of Norwich, Henry de Spenser, who had a well armed professional army showed no respect for the building and he had all who were there captured and killed instantly. At North Walsham there is a cross which marks the site of the battle. (See page 22)

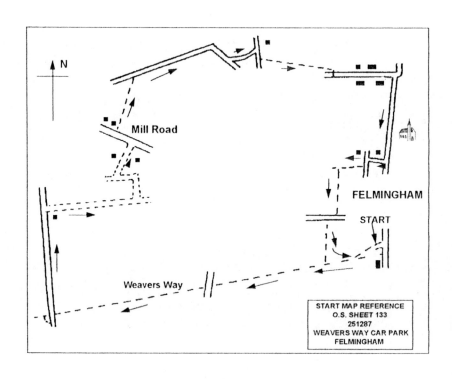

N

Mill Road

FELMINGHAM

START

Weavers Way

START MAP REFERENCE
O.S. SHEET 133
251287
WEAVERS WAY CAR PARK
FELMINGHAM

19

NORTH WALSHAM

4 MILES

The free Weavers Way car park is situated in Station Road which is on the outskirts of the town. The entrance to Station Road is off the Aylsham Road opposite the entrance to Walls Engineering. There are several places in North Walsham that serve good food.

START WALK From the car park go towards the notice boards and turn left at the junction of paths. Go through the gate, cross road and take the footpath that runs parallel to the road on the right-hand side of it.

At T junction of paths turn right then fork left along the narrow path between fence and hedge. It then goes alongside a playing field. Go under the railway bridge and turn left onto a concrete path.

Cross main road and turn right going under the road bridge. Continue along pavement walking into North Walsham, passing thatched cottages and further along the Angel Bookshop.

At cross roads with traffic lights turn right, passing The Feathers on right. Bear right and aim for the Market Cross.

The Market Cross was built by Bishop Thirlby who was Lord of the Manor of North Walsham, in 1549. A fire destroyed it and in 1600 it was rebuilt by Bishop Redman. At first it was used as a toll house, later it became known as the 'Town Clock'. This was put there by John Juler, a watchmaker, in 1787. In 1897 the Market Cross was restored again. It is now a listed building. The drinking fountain was erected to commemorate the coronation of King George V.

Continue along this attractive street. The 13th century church on left is well worth visiting. Work on the building was interrupted by the 'Black Death' plague in 1348; the fatal epidemic killed many of the skilled craftsman. Some of the gems to be seen in this lovely church are the 15th century font, and the screen, of which only the dado (base panels) remain, they are of exceptional 15th century design.

At the end of New Road turn right, turn right again into Grammar School Road, passing Paston School 6th Form College on right. The school was founded by Sir William Paston in 1765. The present building was built on the site of the old house. One of its most famous pupils was Horatio Nelson, who left the school in 1771 to join the crew of HMS 'Raisonable' and there to begin his famous naval career.

The pavement bears left to the A149. Cross this road at crossing and continue along the Norwich Road going under the railway bridge. Along this road there stand a variety of Victorian houses.

Just after the entrance to a wide track stands a stone marking the site of the Peasants Revolt in 1381.

Turn right into the wide track with water towers on left. At the end of the track by footpath sign walk diagonally across field on well defined path. With pond on far right continue to hedge line.

Over these fields deer roam and in winter time their cloven footprints can be seen in the soil.

Take the path straight ahead keeping the hedge on your right. Continue along the field edge to track and turn along it.

The footpath at end of track crosses into the field on your left. Turn right and keep beside the field edge with hedge on right. Follow direction of footpath sign situated at the end of bank with two trees.

Go diagonally right across field aiming for corner of the wood. Take path through the edge of the wood. It then continues at edge of field. Turn left at footpath sign along another edge of field keeping the wood on left. Cross road and go down country lane opposite with another wood on left.

Just before railway bridge turn left up steps then turn right along old railway track - Weavers Way. Continue along this path. Cross road and go along path opposite. Turn left into car park and start of walk.

This old railway track is now a haven for wild life. On of the wild flowers to be found is hawkweed, a tall plant with purple florets. In days gone by it was used for healing wounds. Honeysuckle winds itself around bushes and trees, another name for it is woodbine, sometimes it coils around trees and deforms them. It is another plant that was used to heal, this time for headaches, lung problems and asthma. The dog rose also spreads itself over the bushes and hedgerow. Generations of children in the past were brought up on the syrup made from the hips as they contain vitamin C.

Trees such as the rowan with its bright red poisonous berries grow along here, it is said to keep witches away and that is the reason many country folk had them growing in their gardens.

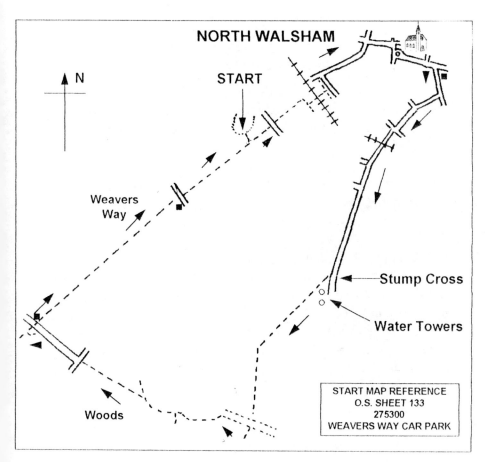

NORTH WALSHAM

N

START

Weavers
Way

Stump Cross

Water Towers

START MAP REFERENCE
O.S. SHEET 133
275300
WEAVERS WAY CAR PARK

Woods

24

HONING & DILHAM

6 MILES

This is a very pleasant route through woodland. and beside the old Dilham canal. There is limited parking at the road junction at Lock Road, Honing which is situated on a minor road 2 miles northeast of Worstead.

START WALK Go along Lock Road passing houses on right. The road becomes a rough track. Turn left along Weavers Way just after the houses and just before concrete gate posts.

Go along this tree lined track which is attractive all year round. In autumn the bracken and the trees are golden in colour. In Spring gorse with its bright yellow flowers grows along here. Broom also flourishes and is very similar to gorse but does not have spines. Among the wild flowers are the white dead nettle, so named because the leaves do not sting when they are touched and the pink flower of the rosebay willowherb, a tall plant whose downy white seeds are scattered by the wind in autumn.

Ignore paths to right and left. Further along there are ponds either side of the path. Go through gate and leaving Weavers Way turn right at lane with footpaths sign. Go through gate and continue along path between meadows. Please keep dogs on leads here as sheep and cattle graze these meadows.

Climb two stiles after the second stile walk along field edge to bank. Turn left along bank beside the old Dilham canal. This canal was built in 1820. It was 8 miles long and had 6 locks and 8 bridges. It was built for the local people who were fed up with exorbitant tolls charged on the turn pike roads.

It closed in 1930, however in 1982 a local landowner and other bodies restored the canal and Anglian Water agreed to stop pumping sewage into it! Today kingfishers, moorhen, ducks and swans and geese can be seen in and around the canal.

Climb stiles and go over bridge and along rough track. Turn left along a wide hedged and tree lined track. Ignore footpath to right. Just past the keepers cottage on right the track becomes a country lane.

Turn left. To the left Dilham staithe can be seen. Turn right into Honing Road. (If you wish to visit the Cross Keys Inn in The Street turn left for about 500 yards. They have an extensive menu plus several real ales to offer the weary traveller. Retrace steps.)

Along Honing Road turn left at footpath sign and go through gate. Keep the bank on right at the edge of the field and keep straight ahead to track. Turn right along it to road.

Cross road and go along lane opposite with church on right. Where the lane bears left turn right along track, it bears left further along. Follow field edge right then left to road.

Turn right at country lane then left down a wide track with a house on right. Climb stile and go across meadow to wood. Keeping wood close on left and just before the canal turn left climbing stile and going over plank bridge. Continue along woodland path going over plank bridges.

The path turns right over a lock bridge. Continue along this path and over plank bridge and at track turn left and immediately left again along Weavers Way. At country lane turn left between wood and common.

Walk through Honing village and at road junction go straight across to footpath sign and follow path to the church.

This lovely old church is worth a moment of your time. It has a slim and high perpendicular tower and a 13th century stone carved font amongst its gems. Go through churchyard keeping church on left.

Cross road and continue along footpath opposite. At track turn right. (Ignore footpath to left) At the road turn left.

Turn right into Common Road and left at 'The Cottage' back to start of walk.

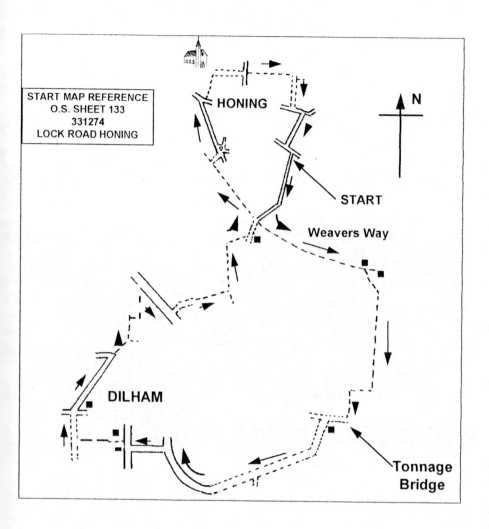

START MAP REFERENCE
O.S. SHEET 133
331274
LOCK ROAD HONING

HONING

N

START

Weavers Way

DILHAM

Tonnage
Bridge

POTTER HEIGHAM

5 MILES

This Broads walk starts at the lovely thatched church with its 12th century round tower. There is parking available on the green by the church. To reach the church drive along Station Road and turn right into Church Lane. There are no pubs on route. However Potter Heigham has three pubs the Broad Haven Hotel, Falgate Inn and Cringles.

START WALK Go along Marsh Road with church on your left. Turn right at the footpath sign; the path becomes a rough track between wet meadows.

In the ditches common reed grows profusely. It is one of Britain's tallest grasses and makes ideal thatching material. Swans can be spotted on the wet meadows and skylarks can be seen several hundred feet above the grassland singing their clear warbling song.

The skylarks plumage is brown and the bird is often hard to spot when on the ground.

At T junction of tracks turn left. Ignore the footpaths to left over footbridge and continue along the track. Turn left at the second bridge and climb steps. Turn right along bank path for a short distance, here Candle Dyke links into Hickling Broad.

Many different species of water birds can be seen here, and eels and other fish live in the water. On posts on the far left cormorants sit. These large birds are members of the pelican family. Marsh harriers have been spotted and geese and duck fly over the marshes to land on the water where crested grebes are a familiar sight.

Go back along the path to the steps at the top of the bridge and continue along the bank going down steps with entrance to the thatched house on right.

This is a conservation area. The other birds that can be heard and spotted amongst the reed beds are the reed and sedge warbler and the reed bunting with its black head and throat.

Ignore path to left where Weavers Way joins the path. Further along pause at the hide (Please remember to shut the hide flaps on leaving) On the far expanse of water many other water birds can be spotted including shell duck, moorhen and coot. The difference between the two latter birds is mainly the first has a red bill base and the coot a white bill and forehead.

Ignore another path to left and continue along the main path. Climb stile and turn right along country lane. Just past Decoy Lodge turn left at footpath sign up a drive and then between hedge and greenhouse. Go through gap and cross the field, keeping by the bank on left if it has not now been removed altogether! Half way across the bank should be on your right, however aim for the footpath sign in front of pink cottage at the far end of the field.

Turn right at the country lane then soon left into Green Lane. Turn left along a narrow path between houses with yellow marker sign. Turn left along Chapel Road with its pretty cottages and at its end turn right at yellow marker sign along the field edge.

Turn left at country lane. Further along leave the lane at footpath sign on right and go diagonally across the field on defined path, (Potter Heigham church can be clearly seen) go through hedge gap and continue along the defined path across second field. Turn right at road and walk back to start of walk at church.

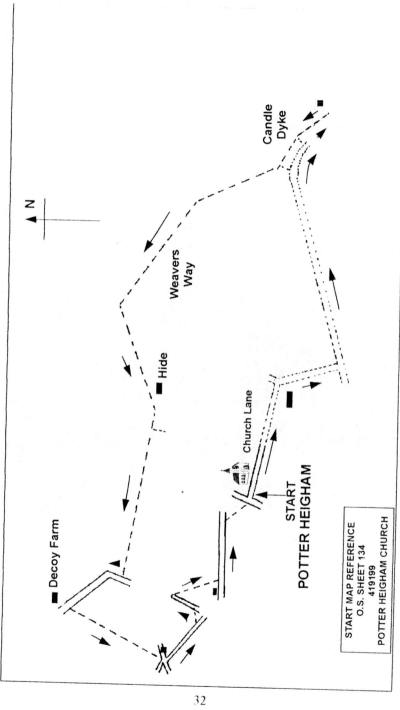

N

Decoy Farm

Weavers
Way

Hide

Candle
Dyke

Church Lane

START
POTTER HEIGHAM

START MAP REFERENCE
O.S. SHEET 134
419199
POTTER HEIGHAM CHURCH

POTTER HEIGHAM BRIDGE & THURNE VILLAGE

5 1/2 MILES

This walk is a very pleasant one beside the River Thurne and around the Broads, even on a misty day in winter! There is parking at Potter Heigham Bridge, but in season it is not a free one.

START WALK Go over the bridge and opposite the Amusement 'shop' turn right along Weavers Way keeping the River Thurne on right. The path goes behind holiday chalets for a while. Continue along this path until you reach Thurne 19th century Drainage Mill.

The river is a busy one with boats of all shapes and sizes in spring and summer. Herons, great crested grebes, ducks and geese are found on the river. Kestrels hover over the meadows. In spring and summer wild flowers grow on the bank, their various colours brightening the path such as the yellow flowers of the ox-tongue, pink flowers of the hemp-agrimony and bright white flowers of the convolvulus.

Reaching the mill the path turns left alongside the staithe, which is an Anglo/Saxon word for landing place. At the end of the staithe is the Lion Inn, a very friendly place where an extensive menu and real ales are served.

Turn left along the country lane walking through the pretty village of Thurne. Pass a turn to the right. Turn right at the T junction and go along the public footpath. This path becomes a wide grass one. Just before the entrance to the farm turn left at footpath sign and go through gate.

Keep along path with wood on left. This is a favourite spot for dragon flies and rosebay willowherb gives a dash of colour with its pink flower and long green leaves.

Go through gateway and over footbridge. Cross second footbridge and continue along field edge. At the end of the hedge line go across field on defined path. Cross road and continue along the footpath opposite. Go to the right of the gate along good path at field edge. Continue across field on defined path.

Cross track and keep along footpath at edge of field and allotments. Turn left along the country lane opposite a lovely old thatched cottage. At the main road turn left along it, then keep left along the minor road back to start of walk.

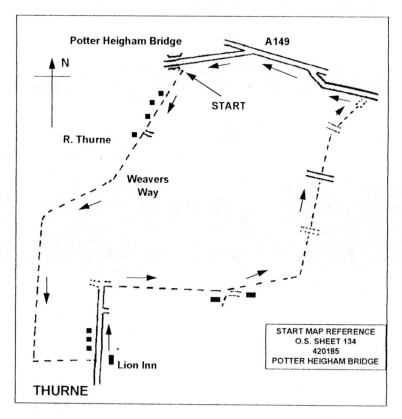

ACLE

5 1/2 MILES

This a lovely easy walk around the Broads, Weavers Way and the River Bure. It starts from Acle's free car park which is off Bridewell Lane behind the new Methodist Church

START WALK From the car park go back to Bridewell Lane and turn right. Turn right into Pyebush Lane. The path bears left and becomes a rough track then goes at the edge of a field.

The path bears right and continues on a well defined path between fields. Cross lane by the church with its round tower. Go along the footpath opposite on another well defined path between crops. Over these fields, pheasants and partridge can be seen.

This path continues along a hedged lane. At the road bear right towards The Green. Keep straight ahead along Horses Head Lane passing a lovely old house with pond on right.

The road becomes a track and winds right and left by ditches. Just before crossing a ditch turn right by yellow marker sign along a narrow path keeping the wide ditch on left. Cross narrow iron bridge and continue along path through meadow.

Climb stiles. later cross track and take the footpath opposite with footpath sign. Continue along this path to the river. Climb bank and turn right keeping the River Bure and chalets on left.

In summer this river is alive with colourful river craft. In winter it is a peaceful solitary place to walk and spot the wintering birds on the river.

Keep along the path through the boatyard with the Horizon Craft building on your right. Cross main road and turn right along drive to the Bridge Inn. Keep close to the left hand side of the Inn and follow the path to the river.

The Bridge Inn is a friendly place and welcomes walkers. It offers tasty meals as well as good beer.

This Weavers Way path is at first on the far side of the reed beds away from the river and then follows close beside the river itself. Climb stiles. The path turns right leaving the river and going beside Acle Dyke.

Climb stile, cross track and follow the Weavers Way sign. The path goes along a rough tree lined track. Cross the busy main road and continue along the footpath opposite. Cross railway line with care, **STOP-LOOK-& LISTEN** and continue along the wide grass path.

At the junction with a rough track turn right over a bridge. The track becomes a tarmac one. Turn right at road junction into Acle. Go under bridges passing St. Edmunds Church with its thatched roof and round tower.

Go straight across the junction keeping the thatched house on left and the Acle sign on right. Continue along the road and turn right into Bridewell Lane then left by the Methodist Church back to the car park and start of walk.

In the 13th century Acle was granted market status. In its hey-day farmers drove their cattle over the Reedham Ferry to attend the auctions, rabbits and chicken were also sold. Today the market is held on Thursdays and it's a very popular affair.

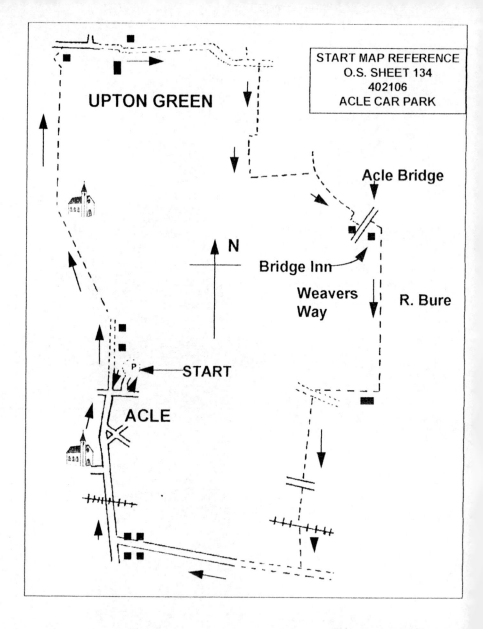

START MAP REFERENCE
O.S. SHEET 134
402106
ACLE CAR PARK

UPTON GREEN

Acle Bridge

N

Bridge Inn

Weavers
Way

R. Bure

START

ACLE

HALVERGATE

9 1/2 MILES

This is a lovely walk with panoramic views of the low lying countryside on the whole of this walk, where in winter migrating birds feed. There is free parking at the church in Halvergate which is situated 2 miles south of the A47 between Acle & Great Yarmouth.

START WALK Keeping the church behind you, walk towards the attractive village sign keeping to the left along Sandhole Road. Turn right into Marsh Road. Weavers Way joins this road. Continue along it passing the Red Lion, it serves food, but not on Sundays,and real ale.

Alexanders with their yellow flowers grow in the banks in spring. This herb was named after Alexander the Great. The whole of it is edible. The green leaves help to make a tasty white sauce. the young stems can be eaten like asparagus; the flower buds used in salads and the roots as a vegetable because they taste like parsnips.

As the road bends left turn right up track with Weavers Way sign. Go through gate keeping along the Fleet Dyke path and ignoring path to right.
A member of the thrush family, the fieldfare is a winter visitor and can be spotted on the meadows as well as barn owls, swans and golden plovers.

Climb stiles and keep along the grass path following the Weavers Way sign. At the concrete track turn right with Weavers Way sign. Cross railway line with care - **STOPPING - LOOKING & LISTENING.**

Turn right and climb stile. The 366 acres of the Berney Marshes are owned by the R.S.P.B. Keep to the path on top of the Breydon Water bank. It is here that the Rivers Waveney and Yare meet.

On the water cormorants and shell duck can be seen, and in the ditches coot and kingfishers can be spotted.

Climb stile. Pass the Berney Arms on your right. This pub is only open from Easter to October. It serves good food and a choice of real ales. The 19th century drainage mill has a seventy foot tower

Just after the mill turn right, go down steps and climb stile. At first bear right along track but keep to the left of the electricity poles leaving the main track. Go through gate and cross meadow. Go through wooden gate and cross meadow. Go through wooden gate and aim for white gates. Go through white gates and cross railway line again - **STOPPING - LOOKING & LISTENING.**

Go through wooden gate and cross meadow, following the Weavers Way sign. Go through metal gate and turn left over earth bridge and through second gate and continue over meadow with ditch on right.   ,

Turn right and go over bridge. Bear left over meadow keeping the windpump straight ahead. Go through gateway and across meadow. Go through gate or cross the plank bridge and turn left at track.

Ignore path to right and continue along wide grass path. Reed bunting can be spotted in the reeds and red admiral butterflies and their 'offspring' black caterpillars, on the nettle leaves.

The path becomes a concrete one and bears right.

The route passes the lovely Wickhampton Church which has several wall paintings that are well preserved and many other gems such as the gruesome story of the two brothers who owned land in the villages of 'Wicked-Hampton & Hell-Fire-Gate' (Wickhampton & Halvergate.)

They disputed so strongly about their boundaries that they quarrelled and fought until they took each others heart out. God manifested his displeasure at such a cruel conduct by turning the brothers into stone and with their hearts in their hands they were placed in the church to deter others from a similar act of wickedness.

Go past the thatched cottages and keep straight ahead at road junction. Turn right along the country lane.

After the playing field and Halvergate Hall and opposite a thatched cottage turn left. Continue along this road passing the village sign back to start of walk.

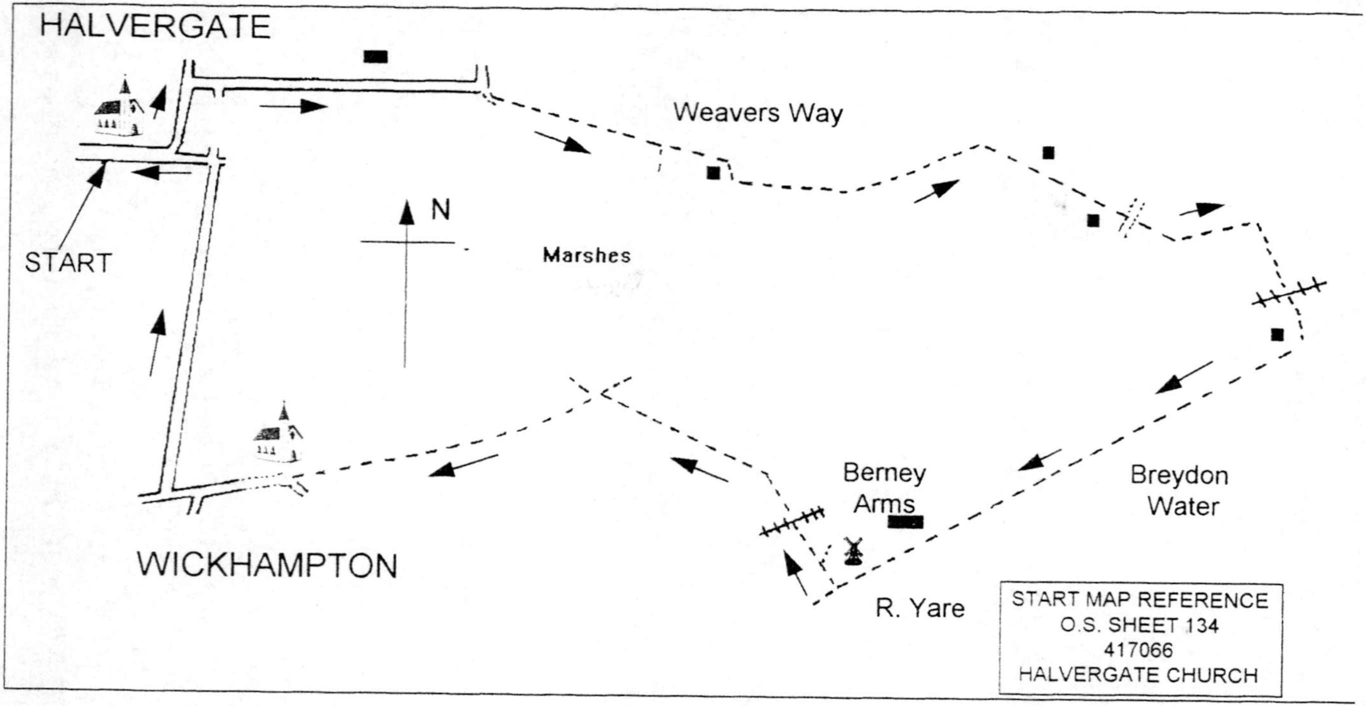

HALVERGATE

Weavers Way

Marshes

N

START

WICKHAMPTON

Berney Arms

Breydon Water

R. Yare

START MAP REFERENCE
O.S. SHEET 134
417066
HALVERGATE CHURCH

43

GREAT YARMOUTH

3 1/2 MILES

This a a pleasant walk around the rivers Yare (pronounced 'Yeah') and Bure. This first part is excellent for watching waders and other birds. There is no pub en-route, but there are plenty of places in and around Great Yarmouth to take refreshments. There is parking available at the railway station.

START WALK Keeping the railway station on right make your way to the road and cross it. Go along path with river on left passing the large ASDA sign.

Keep along Weavers Way riverside path passing a hide on left with railway lines on right. Cormorants can be seen sitting on posts out on the water and flocks of goldfinches feeding at the tide mark of the river.

Keep along this path climbing stiles and with the Breydon Water hide on left. Here there are a multiplicity of waders to be spotted feeding as well as shell duck and oyster catchers.

Go through gates and climb stile then go down bank on right onto track and cross the railway line with care, once again - **STOPPING - LOOKING & LISTENING!** Go along track to another gate and **again cross railway line with care.** Continue along the track and go through gate.

Cross main road and turn right and walk along the verge. Turn left at footpath sign along Paddy's Loke. Keep along this grassy path between wet meadows where swans can be seen and a ruined windmill. The path becomes a tarmac one between offices. At T junction turn right keeping the River Bure on left.

Keep along the North River Road. It curves and finally reaches the dual carriageway. Cross this road, turn right and then left through stone bollards back to the station and start of walk.

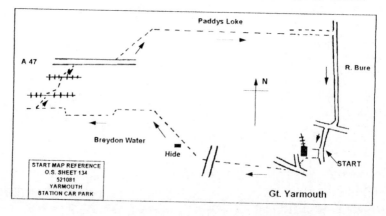

Joy & Charles Boldero came to live in Norfolk in 1983. Being experienced walkers they decided to publish their own walk books containing walks around Norfolk. (See list in front of book).

They have also compiled walks for North Norfolk District Council, Broadland District Council and the Norfolk County Council. The walks in the A.A. publication "Leisure Guide to East Anglia" were written by them and they wrote walks for a national magazine "Out & About" covering Norfolk and South Lincolnshire.

They write the weekly walk which appears in the Eastern Daily Press Saturday's Magazine. It appears on the inside of the back page. The walks are written in their very special style which makes the walk an interesting article not only for the many walkers who follow their column and complete the walks, but also for those who follow the route from their 'arm chairs'! They cover the whole of Norfolk and sometimes go over the border into Suffolk and Cambridgeshire. In 1993 they acted as Walk Guides for the Norfolk Adult Education Service during the summer months.
Their golden retriever Tammy, accompanies them on all their walks.

Joy & Charles Boldero also give walk/slide talks about walking in Norfolk and its countryside.

All their walks take the walker mostly over public footpaths. bridleways and tracks with a good hostelry (Pub or Inn) recommended for a welcome pint of real ale and good food.
The book also includes details of the old uses of some of the wild flowers that can be found in the banks and hedges. It names some of the birds, such as avocets and marsh harrier that can be spotted in the marshes and creeks; and it gives historic information regarding the places visited on the walks.

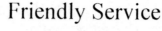